I0170108

Civilized Ways

Gary Beck

Winter Goose Publishing

This publication is a creative work protected in full by all applicable copyright laws, as well as by misappropriation, trade secret, unfair competition, and other applicable laws. No part of this book may be reproduced or transmitted in any manner without written permission from Winter Goose Publishing, except in the case of brief quotations embodied in critical articles or reviews. All rights reserved.

Winter Goose Publishing
2701 Del Paso Road, 130-92
Sacramento, CA 95835

www.wintergoosepublishing.com
Contact Information: info@wintergoosepublishing.com

Civilized Ways

COPYRIGHT © 2014 by Gary Beck

First Edition, December 2014

Cover Art by Winter Goose Publishing
Typeset by Odyssey Books

ISBN: 978-1-941058-22-0

Published in the United States of America

Indomptablement a dû
Comme non espoir s'y lance
Éclater là-haut perdu
Avec furie et silence.

"Petit air"—Stéphane Mallarmé

Table of Contents

The more American poets I read the less connected I felt to their concept of poetry, however much I admired their artistic accomplishments. I saw a world aflame with constant upheavals, disasters man-made or natural, and progressively more destructive violence. Yet I found poets increasingly seeking esoteric metaphors, cherishing style above substance, placing form above content . . . My poetry began to reflect the broader range of world problems, with the subject being my primary concern, not the expression thereof. This further distanced me from the practitioners of the art of poetry.

"An Assertion of Poetry"—Gary Beck

To Nancy,
a bright light that does not dim,
despite the darkness that always threatens to engulf us

The Dance of Hate

To David N. Dinkins

The dance of hatred that we spin
turns one group against another,
chooses rage instead of tolerance,
as blood speaks louder than reason.

The voices of dissension
seek violent solutions,
since it's easier to kill
than to get along.

The endless dance of confrontation
pairs fanatical antagonists,
dedicated to rejection
of sensible compromise.

Palestinian suicide bombers
recruited from the dispossessed,
sent by ruthless calculators,
who save themselves for middle-class comforts.

The Orangemen march and bang their drums,
flaunting unforgotten victories
over countrymen who look alike,
but fear each other's house of worship.

The Buddhists pray and sound their gongs
when communists come to arrest them
for rejecting the state religion
that requires soulless obedience.

The Moslem cries to animists
that one god only is allowed
and will slaughter unbelievers
who don't accept the one true god.

So Islam wars against other faiths
in Israel, Sudan, Nigeria,
while Central Europe and the Balkans seethe,
and the Arab street reviles the Great Satan.

It seems that human destiny
builds armies of extermination
that dance the dance of endless strife,
fertilize blossoms of destruction.

Train Ride

I barely got aboard
when wheels began to roll,
racing along rattling tracks
piercing the bowels of the city.

I lurched from car to car
searching for an empty seat,
my choice a car of squalling brats,
or toxic clouds of the smoking car.

Breathing's more important than deafness,
so I picked the chamber of shrieks,
concealing myself in a book,
while thinking of the bullet train.

We were still in the tunnel,
dim lights revealing toiling serfs,
the city's underground search crews
seeking the subterranean homeless.

Then we burst into the light, the light
the babies yowled, the moms howled,
in the confines of the Pullman car
infant arias were corrosive.

A few minutes passed in the long trip,
the train rolling south on viewless route
of blank walls, patchy shrubbery,
more bearable than travelers' faces.

The hours crept by on resentful toes
that thwarted my efforts for tolerance.
The volume level of cows and calves
clarified why bulls were solitary.

Darkness fell. The illusion of the window
faded, my stressed face looking back at me.
I could not focus on my book,
held hostage by overwhelmed senses.

I closed my eyes but couldn't obliterate
snorts and rumbles of the grazing herd,
and yearned for ability
to pass time in meditation.

Crotchety time hated to pass,
as I rode this train of doom
much longer than intended,
trapped in lethal container.

I rose, but was quickly skewered
by inquisitor's eyes, stabbing suspicions.
They know I'm a poet! Can I deny it?
Does it matter? Should I fear punishment?

I carefully traversed sprawl of legs,
luggage, coats, baby food, rattles, debris
of tribal movement of Hussites,
or another alien horde.

Wary glances followed me.
I couldn't go far, or they'd open my suitcase
and find incendiary poems . . .
Ah. That's nonsense. They wouldn't care about poems.

I took a deep breath for reassurance,
with spring in my step, friendly smile,
I showed the eternal conductor
my ticket of continuation.

The rest of the trip passed quietly.
I forgot apprehensions,
took my place in the migration,
arrived at my destination.

Proximity bred familiarity,
my fellow voyagers waved farewell
as I detrained at a rural station,
leaving good will, taking theirs.

Mutilated Girls

Decorated veterans of Brazil's harsh slums
the street girls who sleep on park benches,
fall drugged on sidewalks,
drunkenly sell sex at tourist bars,
slash their arms with razor blades,
scars the bitter emblems of their lives.

Dumped on the streets as children
the girls survive by being tough,
not just against potential molesters,
but by enduring trials of life,
the fiercest girls most scarred,
stripes earned in the army of the streets.

Their wounds a compulsive reminder
of unrelenting abuse on the streets,
their scars warning the threatening world:
"I'm capable of cutting me,
so I'm capable of cutting you.
I'm not decent anymore,
rape, prostitution, disease
have tainted me beyond redemption.
My brief, turbulent life is recorded
in slashes carved in my polluted flesh.
They'll never go away."

Lest We Forget

For many years
the faults
of our tormented country
made us forget
the big heart of America,
as we allowed greed
to pervade the land.
That fateful day,
September 11th, 2001,
that should be remembered
in this world of hatred,
because those toppled towers
were not Babel,
but an international trading post,
preserving civilization
from implacable assailants.
In the aftermath
heroes gave their lives
saving others,
volunteers rushed in,
Americans opened their wallets
to sustain others,
as we were reminded by history
that no other country
has been so generous.

Child Soldiers

Children of the AK-47
your brief lives will be ended,
as soon as your cartridges
have been expended.

Unlike warriors of old
who trained in the ways of war,
child soldiers pick up their guns
younger than ever before.

The nurturing machinegun sings
the only soothing lullaby
that urchin armies ever hear
in their last moments as they die.

When children's bones are bleaching white
in the skeleton dance of time,
adults who made these infants kill
were the true authors of the crime.

Their stunted bodies line the road,
victims of the endless strife,
kissed goodbye by the bullets,
that end their futile life.

America

To Ralph Nader

Once America was bountiful,
except in times of famine.
The limited number of humans
were insufficient to destroy the land.
Small tribes migrated from Asia,
hunted, fished, grew a little corn,
but in the abundance of the land
didn't use much. Neither did they ruin
everything for everyone else.
The Indians weren't particularly noble,
or dreadfully savage, compared to other invaders
like the Europeans, who came to unspoiled shores
with gifts of greed, disease, destruction,
stored in the hulls of their bold ships.

And the heirs of America, sons and daughters
who never learned their duty to nature,
blind to the needs of the future,
poured enough concrete to smother the earth,
spread poisonous chemicals
that pollute our air and water
so the lords of profit can flourish.
Perhaps someday, before it is too late,
our clever science will find a way
to make toxic water drinkable,
tainted air breathable.
Now it is beyond our scope and means
to ensure the children of tomorrow
will be sustained in this fragile life,
on this much abused land.

Children at War

When I was a boy
Myanmar wasn't a country,
so how could they do anything wrong,
if they didn't exist?
Their army dragged children off the streets
and used their bodies as minesweepers.

In Sri Lanka,
another country that didn't exist
when I was a boy,
young Tamil girls,
fondly named "Birds of Freedom,"
were trained as suicide bombers.

I think Iraq existed
when I was a boy,
but now it's a malignant dwarf.
And while America fretted
about gays infiltrating the Boy Scouts,
Saddam's "Lion Cubs" earned small-arms merit badges.

Thousands and thousands of children
are fighting and dying in dozens of wars,
that when I was a boy
didn't seem to expend them
as spies, sentries, servants, sex slaves,
but now they're a cheap commodity.

September 11th, 2001

The surprise terrorist attack
made a ghost
of the twin towers.

The hijacked planes contained
unwary travelers,
innocently in flight.

They were cruelly condemned
without a trial
and flown to their deaths.

Those tall spires received
unwarranted destruction
they couldn't escape.

The planes plunged into walls
not strong enough
to deflect missiles.

And the workers fled,
those who could,
but not three thousand.

Many jumped from windows,
forced to choose
between leaping or burning.

Police and firefighters
rushed inside with dedication
and saved many lives.

But then the walls came down
and the brave
perished with everyone else.

First one proud tower fell,
then the second
a heartbreak later.

The dust and crash concealed
the ravaged bodies
of those who didn't escape.

As we watched in horror,
Arabs danced for joy
at our pain and suffering.

We were dazed for a while,
then the questions began,
business went back to normal.

Squabbles over money
took shameful precedence
over efforts to revere the lost.

We still have a chance
to oppose the terror
that fuels hatred in the world.

We shouldn't forget our loss
and treat terror
as we would rabid dogs.

Murdered Children

Two children took a trip one day,
to State Supreme Court in the Bronx,
and told how Mother and Father
murdered their four-year-old sister.

They shyly spoke in muffled words
of relentless years of abuse
suffered in their cruel apartment,
that now happens everywhere.

They talked of terrible torture,
being tied to chairs and beaten,
burned with cigarettes, or matches,
their sister, S., suffered the worst.

Parents beat their daughter to death.
Later the little children swore
that S. was always hardest hit,
was most hated and called ugly.

S. was tied to a chair at night,
little bones curled to the plastic,
not allowed to use the bathroom,
punished for wetting herself.

A. witnessed her sister's murder,
a bloody room-to-room journey
that began in the bathroom,
because S. drank from the toilet.

Both parents beat S.
in the bathroom, the living room,
finished her off in the kitchen,
leaving her dead on the table.

J. was the first to testify,
a graphic seven-year-old's tale.
Her mother warned her to shut up,
or she'd get the same as S.

J. described her own injuries,
beaten, burned with cigarettes,
burned with a hair curling iron,
tied to a chair for the night.

R. was next to testify
and told the judge he would not lie.
He tightly clutched his *Star Trek* figure,
lost in his over-sized jacket.

R. told the same tale of horror
told by his two sisters:
Mommy and Daddy beating S.,
because she always made them mad.

When the testimony ended
the children were still doubted,
vulnerable witnesses
trapped in a world of despair.

The children left the courtroom
with their lawyer, eating candy,
little bodies undernourished.
Mother blew kisses goodbye.

Mother took the witness stand,
a troubling inhuman face,
nervous from lack of cocaine.
She wouldn't be mother of the year.

She's trapped in an endless cycle
of violence, cruel abuse,
her children unprotected
in our crumbling culture.

Democracy

To Ted Weiss

One burden of democracy
is the confusion it creates
for its citizenry,
who don't recognize the fragility
of an arbitrary system.

The drone who runs his motorboat
on a still lake,
exercising his right to pollute
with oil, gas, other toxins,
until only a motorboat survives.

The rustic man who slaughters sparrows
in a murderous spree to save the bluebirds
already doomed to loss of habitat
by mindless, profitable construction
without regard to consequence.

Protesters against globalization
who may or may not be sincere,
but shriek passionate objections
louder than the serfs of eld
resisting feudalism.

O wonderful democracy
that nurtures slick exploiters
who clamor for meritocracy
in a consumer based society
that is exhausting merit.

Miner's Quest

To Don Petersen

And the miners came down from the hills
only once a month, to eat, drink, fight,
if they were lucky,
spend the night with a woman,
instead of in jail.
For Sheriff Bennett met them at the edge of town
and gave them the same warning each time:
"Have a good time, boys, but don't wreck the town."
And the miners nodded sincerely,
chorused, "Sure, Sheriff. You bet. We promise."

But the sheriff was used to their rough ways
and knew they were there to escape the pressures
that gripped them in the bowels of the earth.
And they weren't bad men, just childlike,
toiling like slaves of eld, then seeking release.
They meant their promises and meant no harm.
Nevertheless, the sheriff hired extra deputies
on the day the miners came to town
for their monthly binge.

Now the miners respected the sheriff,
who understood their need to blow off steam,
but the deputies were another kind of cop.
Mostly young, scared, acting tough to impress the hard men
who only feared Mother Earth's crushing embrace
waiting to hold them close, far beneath the surface.
And they mocked the posing deputies
who wore mirrored sunglasses to hide the uncertainty
that made the miners mistrust them.

There was one deputy the miners really hated.
Reardon, a big-bellied bully, meaner than the rattlesnakes
that sometimes tumbled down the mineshaft
and couldn't find their way to the surface again
and shared the dark confines with their fellow prisoners
and sometimes got lucky and bit someone,
before the miners could stomp them to death.
The only thing the miners hated more than rattlers
were the bosses, whose venom flowed from far away.

Reardon always greeted them the same way,
slapping his club in his bulbous paw, scaring no one,
but alert for the chance to hurt the miners.
They despised him, staring through him,
another dangerous clod of earth to be avoided,
but never feared, because he only trapped the unwary,
and if you labored deep below the ravaged earth
you learned to be wary, or didn't survive
the hungry pits that always beckoned.

So the miners rushed to their favorite bars,
where bored trailer girls served the drinks
and didn't really care that a lot of hands
did a lot of exploring of their veined bodies.
And they listened to the usual comments:
"That's a number one shaft. Deep hole. Dig that strata."
And the girls snapped their gum in boredom,
for they took worse abuse than words
from the harsh hands of their redneck boyfriends.

The retired professor of something or other
met them at Purple Nell's and bought them drinks,
preached to them that they should spare the earth.
They laughed kindly at him and explained it was their job,
if they didn't do it, the company would hire others
eager to take their place in the mines, because
someone was always waiting to steal a man's job.

But they never insulted the professor
while drinking his liquor.

The miners never went to ivy-covered schools,
had no book learning, just blue-collar skill,
acquired the hard way, in the pits of shattered dreams,
where the mines sapped the souls of men
who never got used to the pressing rock above
and the dank, devouring dark below,
always waiting, implacable as time,
to catch a careless miner in a moment's lapse,
the last summons to the final ascent.

A View of New York City

To Michael R. Bloomberg

So how did the Indians
get to Manhattan Island
before the Brooklyn Bridge
allowed rapid transit?

Did they paddle across
the untainted Hudson River
before General Electric
irradiated the fishes?

Did their canoes land safely
in the financial district
before Wall Street carnivores
gobbled up the neighborhood?

Where did the Indians come from?
Brooklyn? Queens? The Bronx? New Jersey?
Though they were called something else then
and had forests instead of concrete.

And what did the Indians do?
Hunt? Pick berries? Invest in real estate?
Set up tourist welcome centers
for the arriving Europeans?

And what about the night life?
Did they spend it snoozing,
because there was no fossil fuel
to light the after-hours clubs?

Then Peter Stuyvesant arrived
and in the most salient fact (after Columbus?)
of grade school education
made the first new world business deal.

Now grade school teachers were a little vague
about the value of the dollar,
but peg-leg Pete got a real bargain
that even included Riker's Island.

We don't hear much more about Indians
because they got in dutch with the new neighbors
and either moved in with their cousins,
or got jobs as traveling wampum salesmen.

The Indians didn't get social benefits
because the Dutch and Brits didn't like welfare
and pioneered the American way . . .
Eliminate what gets in your way.

Murderers of Children

Never again should we ask why,
because they've already slaughtered
too many to question motives.
Now we must decide what to do
about frequent infanticide.
Rational legal procedures
no longer guard the innocent,
trapped in the breakdown of values,
that encourage barbarians
to murder our young citizens.

We urgently need an action plan
that will allow a special task force
to judge the innocence or guilt
of those who murder our children.
This group must have authority,
from the government and governed,
to promptly try infanticides
and execute those found guilty.

The monsters of our brutal culture
violate the prime directive,
preserve and protect our children.
This happens too often for coincidence
in the insane assault on civilization
that requires a suitable response,
or parents will dispose of their offspring
just because they become too demanding.

The money saved from years of trials,
appeals, and long incarceration
can go to outreach and educate
younger and younger parents
not to slaughter their children.

My Prince Hamlet

To Ron Cushing

While I visit Elsinore
the clones of academia
gather in corridors of conformity,
urgent to tear down the humanistic mind.
None of the clamorers of wind
cries, "Behold a great and noble prince."
For if they allowed admiration
they would not be attendant lords,
poor players, nor even jesters.
They would merely be low servants,
hired by the custodians of confusion
to atrophy our sensibilities.

The Good Old USA

Our civil libertarians
civilly resist
infringements on civil rights,
which is good for all of us,
since government by its nature
attracts abusers who seek power
for personal advancement.

We need these libertarians
who defend freedom,
a fragile cloth, easily frayed.
And if they sometimes go too far
to suit some of our values,
we shouldn't forget
they help preserve our liberties.

But now they zealously defend
criminal groups like the Mafia,
who compete vigorously
with corporate and other legitimate crooks
for public and private funds
and the legal right to do business.

So we don't eavesdrop on the Don in prison,
who directs the henchmen
dealing in drugs and violence,
practicing the American way,
which is don't interfere with privacy,
for a man's cell is his castle.

Then terrorists attack our land
and slaughter our people,
and threaten our way of life,
and some put terrorists above the law
that they lust to destroy,
which allows the foes of peace
to continue depredations.

Downy Woodpecker
(Dendrocopos Pubescens)

The Downy Woodpecker,
a surprise resident
of midtown Manhattan,
because some blankety-blank developer
probably demolished
his natural habitat.

So he packed his beak,
shoved off for the big city
with his wife, but no kids,
and they must have leased a nest
somewhere near my terrace,
for they visited daily.

They were a snazzy couple,
dressed alike in black and white,
except he sported a bright red cap.
My wife appreciated them,
providing suet,
winter, spring, and fall.

Then Mrs. Downy disappeared,
perhaps a victim of divorce,
or dead from unknown cause.
Mr. Downy still flies in for suet
three or four times daily,
but faces a constant battle.

Not much larger than a sparrow
and not as rugged,
he confronts a flock of sparrows,
hooligans who have forgotten
his unique occupation,
nature's only working bird.

The Downy eats destructive bugs
from infested city trees,
but gets no respect from sparrows,
who claim the food source for themselves
and bully and chase the weaker birds,
imitating the way of man.

Sparrows are just like people,
consuming as if there is no tomorrow,
demanding larger and larger portions,
while the Downy loses his share
and is forced to search elsewhere
and may never be seen again.

Madre Mia

Sara M., a young immigrant,
illegally came to Brooklyn from Mexico
to find her part of the American dream,
which she shared with Gabriella,
her three-year-old daughter,
who she beat until she died.

Sara M. moved into a nice building,
a lot nicer than the shack in Mexico,
and was thrilled with her own apartment,
but her daughter defecated on the floor,
so she had to be beaten with a stick.

Gabriella was found too late,
unconscious and fatally bruised.
The authorities said she had been long abused.
Her mother entered a guilty plea
to murder in the second degree.

Ode to Man

Let us celebrate together
what we have done together,
for we have depleted
the seas of fishes,
the air of birds,
the land of animals,
only allowing survival
of those we devour.
And those that live despite us,
roach, rat, pigeon,
personal pets,
only comfort us
while we rush to extinction.

Oil and water do not mix,
so the old adage goes,
but we persist in the mixture,
add everything else
to our daily drink,
while we barter away
the air we breathe
for pollution credits.

Disposable Youth

The badly decomposed body
of a young boy was discovered
stuffed in a plastic garbage bag,
near a South Bronx housing project.

The police arrived at nine a.m.
responding to a 9-1-1 emergency call
and found an eighteen-month-old child,
who looked like he had been dead for days.

They hauled the lifeless child away
in a green plastic body bag,
and no one cared, or waved goodbye,
or even knows where the body lies.

Ode to Greed

When the harsh millennia ended
the rhythmic acquisition pulse
throbbed across the eroding globe,
a warning of disasters to come.

In every house, in every hut
from lavish mansion to cardboard box,
the limits of desire are stretched
until the craving nourishes our need.

Child Care

A twenty-eight-year-old mother
pleaded guilty in court
to joining her friends
in torturing her three-year-old son to death,
because he took a piece of candy.

The judge asked the mother
if she heard her boyfriend
and her landlady
beating the child in the bathroom for an hour,
before joining them.

She said she stepped on the boy
with her full weight,
bit him on the arm,
then threw his limp body downstairs.
He died later that evening.

The landlady admitted that she hit the boy
and placed him as punishment
in a tub of ice cold water,
for taking candy.
She was sentenced to two years in prison.

The boyfriend was charged with murder
in the first degree
and he could face the death penalty,
if convicted. The media
didn't bother to report his fate.

Mother avoided the death penalty
by making a full confession
that she tortured the candy thief
for three hours for his crime.
She was sentenced to life in prison.

There is no redemption,
only the lost and devastated lives
that consume the dwindling resources
of a pernicious society,
that no longer protects its young.

To All the Pretenders

I never marched with Martin Luther King,
nor felt the biased teeth of police dogs,
and wasn't washed out of Selma, Alabama,
by high pressure hoses, commanded
by a good-old bull of a sheriff.

I did not ride the freedom train,
nor met the wrathful clubs of summer
that kissed the civil heads of students
asserting the U.S. constitution
should protect us from oppression.

I never frolicked at Woodstock,
nor blew a *J* with a hip chick,
and didn't dance in the rain
in the mythical summer of love,
as the nation throbbed with sex, drugs, rock and roll.

I never served in Vietnam,
nor humped through Uncle Ho's jungles,
didn't slog through punjied paddies,
or hang out in Saigon bars
bragging of forays in the bush.

Pretenders of unearned glory
missed momentous historic events,
resent lack of a role in the drama,
forge wistful tales of the past
that deplete their future.

Hudson River

To George E. Pataki

1. Discovery

Henry Hudson sailed upriver,
then only used by Indians,
who casually shared with fish, fowl, beasts.
How could he foresee, telescoping from his poop deck,
eyeing intimidating forests that concealed the new world,
crammed full of gold, goblins, God knows what,
on that Half Moon, half miracle observation spot,
the hopes, prayers, fears, and lust that propelled the planks
faster than oars, the crew pausing only to commit
the first recorded crimes in the new world,
kidnapping and dispensing liquor to the Indians, without a license.
Although not actually boasting, history takes pride in you
Henry H., obviously overlooking your rough ways
and traditional discoverer's crude exploitation,
for after all you helped introduce civilization.

Then the noble river ran,
clean and pure,
to the untainted sea.

2. Acquisition

The Dutch immigrants neared your shores,
at first intimidated by untamed forests,
then went wild for what they saw
and religiously, six days per week,
began to disrupt animal, vegetable, mineral,
anything interfering with the prompt establishment
of old Amsterdam in New Amsterdam.

They disported on the Sabbath,
cherished kitchen, children, church,
while underfed portraitists, enamored of rosy cheeks,
benevolent glance, and shapely hands,
sanguinely rebrushed their subjects,
eagerly praising the purveyors of power,
the acquirers on the installment plan
of anything they could grab, snatch, ingest, digest,
as they inflicted traditional European values
on fruitful woods, rich earth, endless game,
and only the locals to deal with, fair or foul.
It didn't take long for the colonists to notice
that the Indians lacked friends in high places,
so the inevitable encroachments led to conflict
and burgher housing replaced the wigwam.

Then the noble river ran . . .

3. Colonization

Peter Stuyvesant stumped his city
dreaming a replica of the old world
and gave his loyal follower Joseph Bronck
a reward of a large chunk of the Bronx.
Then the English sailed into the harbor,
and their eyes popped at what they saw,
which they compared to their meager towns.
They promptly evicted the Dutch, who lacked the means
to resist the latest affliction on hospitable shores,
and English quickly shoved the local dialects aside,
spreading the word as fast as the forest fell to hungry axes;
We're here to stay, no matter what you do or say!
The French finally noticed the unruly Brits
and felt their threat to the fur trade,
as well as traditional rivalry and Gallic pride,
sufficient cause to deploy formal European armies.

Of course the distant masters of the new realms
had no idea how to dispute on the vast continent,
so their generals mostly fumbled and bumbled,
alienating the colonists with their haughty ways,
and provoking the Indians to unethical massacres.

Clean and pure . . .

4. Revolution

The leading members of the thirteen colonies
did pretty well for themselves in the new world
and resented the distant rulership of kings.
They evaded or resisted authority,
as the well-to-do always seem to do,
never losing profits during upheavals,
though perhaps regretting the tea lost in Boston harbor.
Finally the armed conflict began
between the colonists and the home government,
and George III was appalled at their ingratitude.
War swirled up and down the Hudson and when it was over,
the sunken ships and cadavers made no impression on you, river.
And the towns and cities on your shores flourished
as fast as the new nation spread beyond the Appalachians.
But ex-mama England was still pining for her lost child
and tested the new owners in a clumsy war
that proved the old order unfit to rule vast America.

To the untainted sea . . .

5. Expansion

So we whipped the British twice, and the Indians,
bought out the French, bluffed the Russians,
finally realized we had a huge land to settle

and opened the shores to white folk of substance.
The shock of shocks was when the barely human Irish
poured in by the thousands, tolerating degradations
just for the chance to grow a few subsistence spuds.
Some of them arrived in time to spill some blood
in the Mexican War, one of our finest land grabs,
that alerted the European powers that the new kid on the block,
puppy America, was voracious for expansion.
And steam began to replace sail to the promised land.
We quickly adopted ex-mama England's industrial revolution,
littering your shores with crude manufactures, river,
and a new class of magnates soared in the North,
disdained, then feared by the agricultural barons of the South.
Invoking the traditional problem-solving method, bloody war,
Americans slaughtered each other while their masters profited.
But enough Irish lost limb or life to claim their fair share
of the delirious promises made by the U.S. Constitution.

Still clean and pure . . .

6. Recovery

Then the soldiers Blue and Gray, weary of the bloody fray,
returned from the uncivil battlefields of decision.
The grateful government pointed the warriors west
for free land, with only pesky Indians in the way,
an easy chore after the rifles of Johnny Reb,
and once across the distant Mississippi
the battle-hardened veterans weren't around
to scrutinize the shady doings in Washington, D.C.
Crouched between your banks, river, you watched industry grow.
The ravaged South began to rebuild, still burdened
by many glances backwards to illusion time,
but others labored mightily to rejoin the present.
This time they crossed you, river, not to return,
and ever westward, in an ever mounting flow,

land-grabbing peasants made their way
across mountains, rivers, deserts, no obstacles allowed
to halt the ravenous spread of manifest destiny.
The puppeteers who make government policy
hired clever propagandists to justify
serious snatching of someone else's property.
Then again, America was founded on larceny.

Still clean . . .

7. Giant Step

We had a lot of new muscle to flex
and the land was pacified from sea to shining . . .
Except for the poor, dispossessed, needy, and disadvantaged,
young America was happy, eager for a worldly role.
Factories sprang up on your shores, Hudson, new enterprises
of small pith and moment, hungry for profits,
discarding failure into your concealing waters.
So our masters looked around for the right adversary
and the decadent Spanish Empire was our lucky choice.
After a minimal investment of blood, limbs, lives,
we snatched Cuba, Puerto Rico, and the Philippines,
and suddenly we were a player on the world scene,
strutting, but not fretting, on the stage of power.
Yet the birds on your shores, river, the fish in your waters,
had no champion to protect their civil rights.
Too late to snatch juicy chunks of Africa or Asia,
young America defended the rights of the colonized,
as long as we could virtuously bark loudly,
but not bite the hands that fed our business.
We watched the big European dogs battle for the bones,
picked the winning side and became a big dog.

The slightly tainted sea . . .

8. Isolation

So we won the first world war, then lost the peace,
bamboozled by those tricky Europeans
into squandering the fruits of victory.
So we picked up our marbles, went home and sulked.
We had a lot of bitter lessons to digest,
until we got bored and conjured up an economic storm
that targeted farmers and laborers,
who were tossed so deep into a depression
that they could not turn their wrathful eyes
on malfeasance in Washington, D.C.,
where officials babbled of a chicken in every pot.
Yet the smokestacks belched profits on your shores, river.
Now that the fertile ground was properly prepared
for the next war of acquisition, all that remained
was the appropriate selection of the candidate enemy.
We considered many choices, but opted for a former friend.
No one else was threatening enough to deny Pacific expansion.
So we sold Japan steel to build ships, planes, tanks,
then cut the oil supply that ran the cherished toys.
And when they came out of the sun that Sunday morning,
we the people screamed foul,
but the lords of profit whispered fair.

Then oil and blood began to taint the sea.

9. Wind-up Cop

Our legions strode across Africa, Asia, Australia,
finally arrived in Europe and crushed the German juggernaut.
Then the sons of the good old USA went home,
renouncing military conquest for college credits.
Meanwhile, the sons of Mother Russia had no tractors,
so they refused to go home and starve on the cold steppes,
and remained in half of Europe, gawking, stealing, replacing the Nazis

with Uncle Joe's version of post-war government,
while Uncle Sam's kids, weary of the years of slaughter,
went back to school to prepare for a better life.
And the corporations gave the ex-G.I.s jobs,
while they dumped their waste in your waters, river.
Yet the lords of profit could have established Pax Americana,
but lacked the will, or balls, or feared the loss of net income.
Instead they sniped at the red menace, dividing countries
that became festering sores on the unhealthy world body,
until one fine June day, half of Korea invaded the other half,
and G.I. Joe was abruptly yanked from the classroom
and sent unprepared, halfway around the world
to fight half an Asian country, without knowing why.
But Uncle Sam said trust me, you have to go,
so our loyal sons dusted off their weapons
and faithfully marched off to war again.

Radiation juices seeped into your waters
and the grateful fishes glowed in the dark.

10. MAD

So we dwindled the not-a-war in Korea,
until the opponents faced each other at the starting point,
where the sons of the red, white, and blue had been fought to a standstill
by the hordes of Genghis Khan, who mocked our legions.
And the national spirit was soured by non-victory.
But the lords of profit achieved their greatest dream,
a standing army that needed endless supplies,
food, shelter, clothing, weapons, wine, women, song,
all provided to Uncle Sugar for top dollar.
And the chemicals were too costly to dispose of,
so PCBs were dumped into your waters, gentle river,
that never surged like the Ohio or the Nile,
that destroyed its helpless neighbors.
And your fish became contaminated,

yet few noticed the toxic assault on your navigable body,
for the times they were a changing and undercitizens
demanded constitutional rights and children of the privileged agreed.
So the lords of profit selected a new Asian diversion
and sent our sons to fight another war with half a country.
Our loyal kids died by the thousands, obediently serving
a terrible cause that was unworthy of their sacrifice.
Yet the coffers of the rich gained as never before,
replacing over and over again, lost planes, tanks, guns, lives.
And when the dying was done and the survivors came home,
no one was held accountable for the bumper crop of body bags.

Chemicals and oil now stain your murky currents.

11. Opiatology

And the legions returned from the "Nam,"
scorned by their fellow Americans
for answering the call to arms,
just like their heroic daddies did.
No welcome-home parades greeted them,
because they betrayed our country
by patriotically serving
in the first war of American defeat.
And the engineers who planned the war
chortled with glee when they got away with murder.
A large dose of public entertainment and comforts
made it easy to eat the flower of forgetfulness,
and renounce the shameful past for the promised dream,
excluding the usual underclass.
For the wealthy have decreed that some must always do without,
so others will appreciate their rank and station.
Then many benefited from democracy
and the sons and daughters of prosperity
forgot their obligations to the nation.
And no one reminded the poisoners

that we all breathe the same air.

Then corporations purchased legislators, river,
who passed laws that allowed the flooding of your waters
with toxins, while the people slumbered.

12. Irresolution

Good old Uncle Sam took it on the chin
from everybody for a while,
until the Wall came tumbling down
and the people danced in the streets.
The lords of profit grimaced
when the lucrative cold war ended
and quickly considered new conflicts.
But doubt had seeped into our genes,
so the right opponent was needed
to divert us from drugs, crime, AIDS, not caring.
We had been kicked out of Africa,
defeated in Southeast Asia,
we were being eased out of Europe
and we couldn't mess with the touchy Latinos.
All that was left was the oil bitch Middle East.
Khadafy was still sulking in his tent,
so the wheel of fortune selected Saddam,
who won the ugliest man in the world contest.
And when our soldiers squashed him a bit,
the simple-minded rejoiced at old-fashioned victory,
despite the paltry opposition,
and awarded the legions a triumph.

The healthiest inhabitants of your waters, river,
old tires, plastic bottles, chemical gunk, used condoms,
race the few remaining fish to the polluted sea.

13. Foreboding

We approached the year 2000, apprehensive
that our computers would not function.
And distracted by our superficial pleasures
in Armani suits and costly imported cars,
we ignored the march of drugs and AIDS
that ravaged our country like plagues of eld.
Now that assembly lines are run by robots
and food is grown in automated fields
and production is controlled by the oppressive few,
the programmers of the world will not unite
to support the endless struggle for liberty,
for they lack the toughness and endurance
for the age-old conflict with the bosses.
Software does not prepare our sons and daughters
for sacrifice on the altar of freedom.
It is too late to resurrect the callused hands and stubborn backs
of farmers, workers, laborers, those accustomed to resist,
although they must always be defeated
by the tyranny of the lords of profit.

The stock market crash of 2015, river,
will fill your waters with the corpses
of those who can't survive loss of comfort.

Children in Combat

Conscripted, cajoled, conned
into volunteering,
often sold by their families
to armies, guerrilla groups, thugs,
children become soldiers, servants, slaves
in increasing numbers
in conflicts that erode the world,
while the trade in small arms
puts big guns in tiny hands.
These undeveloped warriors
do not know school, toys, books,
are well versed in modern weapons,
rights mostly forgotten
in the discharge of automatic rifles.

Madison Square Park

The children's playground reopened
and the happy voices of youngsters
reaffirm the best sound of the city.
Before the park was polluted
by drugs, menacers, violence,
families and singles enjoyed escape
from gasoline streets, stifling rooms
to a small patch of urban green.

Once I brought my daughter to this park,
until our elected guardians
closed the upstate mental institutions,
sent the patients to the big city
without funds, friends, jobs, homes, help,
and the sandbox became the outhouse,
as users squatted in the finest open space
a city can provide, a public park.

Drug peddlers blighted the day,
muggers and sex peddlers stole the night,
until citizens made the effort
to reclaim the park for the people.
They succeeded, things improved,
families returned, singles sit and read,
encouraging us to remember
government alone can't save a park.

Dona Nobis Pacem

When I was young I dreamed
the international brotherhood of man.
I fervently hoped our bombs and bullets
would molder
in the arsenals of death.
But the vision of world peace
did not materialize
in lands of strife and blood,
because my land,
nourished by violence,
would not impose
Pax Americana.

Squalor's Children

See them run,
the skinny-legged kids,
down filthy drug infested streets
bulging with tenements of AIDS,
another uprooted generation,
first white, then black,
now Hispanic, sacrificed
on the altar of profit.

Accruals

Success is a twig
tempting in sunlight,
captured in glassine images
gnarled by implications
that assist pandemonium.
Human engines get exhausted
driving ambition forward
and the shift to cruise control
to maintain acquisitions,
leaves our senses blinded,
lost in Magellanic cloud.

Mad Man

Bruce G. gone completely mad,
angry red beard complaining
sits on sun-touched steps
of a non-comforting church,
menacing the tourists
come to Greenwich Village
to see the odd, peculiar, strange,
even the downright weird,
not the dangerous demented.

Separated by the thinnest line
between unreality and everyone else,
Bruce G. sits and waits for handouts,
unfinished butts, sandwich ends,
does not care who sees, or does not see
as he picks up the discarded refuse,
puffs the cigarette of contamination,
devours the food of contagion
with disinterest in immunity.

Governor C. put Bruce G.
on the train of no return
from a hastily emptied upstate institution.
Bruce G. had a ticket, fifty dollars,
admonitions to take his meds.
Just before Bruce G. got to NYC
Mayor K. closed the SRO hotel
that was supposed to house him,
and he found out that his room
had been converted to a co-op.

Bruce G. is begging on the street,
though that may not have been his choice.
Thank Mayor K. and Governor C.
and those of us who didn't do enough
to force our elected officials,
no longer concerned with the needy
and their commonplace sufferings,
abandoned to the cannibals of compassion,
betrayed by the servants of the people.

Water Foul

We have settled on the shores
of oceans, rivers, lakes, streams,
built our houses on the land's despair,
spilled our contempt on man and nature,
smashed the earth beyond repair,
and poisoned the air and water.
Then having evolved so fast, so far,
we did not think to plan tomorrows.
As savages attack an ancient foe,
relentless in their frenzy,
exulting in the slaughter,
so we inflict our primitive parade
of greedy, blind destruction
on our lady Nature of the sorrows.

The Cold War

To Condoleezza Rice

I first learned about the new kind of war
at age ten, during the Berlin airlift,
when the radio sizzled with praise
for the pilots, who a few years earlier
were busy bombing Berlin.

The newspapers hailed the brave Berliners
who a few years earlier were killing G.I.s,
but reminded us they killed lots of Russians
and now were on the right side at last,
so we forgot old grudges and fed them.

Now I know as well as most of you
that nothing is ever as simple
as the media and our leaders pretend,
and I don't require easy answers,
even though many folk prefer them.

You don't have to know foreign affairs
better than an interior decorator
to know that an iron curtain
is a difficult barrier to open,
and could easily get stuck from rust.

Then our boys were sent to Korea
and it was hard for them to decipher
how the northerners
were different than the southerners,
unless that's the nature of civil war.

But it wasn't civil to our boys
who didn't know why they were there,
fighting up and down a foreign land,
until they finally ended up
right back where they started from.

By this time the Russkies
(I mean the peace loving people
of the Soviet Union)
had built their own A-bombs
in order to equal our peace loving people.

Now this was not diplomacy
like battleship parity,
or agreements not to mobilize armies,
or obeying commands to lay down our muskets.
This was a mad world that invented M.A.D.

First came the long-range bombers,
then the unrecallable missiles,
then the untraceable submarines,
and soon they were ready to party
with the fun-loving people of Cuba.

Now all Fidel had going for him at home
was sugar cane, cigars, and endless rant
in defiance of the good old USA
and he was ready to torch the world
to maintain the communist way.

And our school kids followed instructions
from their deficient school teachers
(who knew nothing about nuclear war)
to hide under their desks
in order to survive nuclear attack.

Huddled beneath their wooden shields
that couldn't even block a dreary curriculum,
the cowering kiddies missed the lesson
that explained that the ostrich defense
was the best our leaders could provide.

But survivalists had a better plan
and trekked to the mountains, excavated caves,
moved in food, water, sleeping bags, radios, guns,
cancelled subscriptions to *The New York Times*
and claimed the right to kill invaders of their hideouts.

And in the suburbs and commuter towns
gardeners planted fallout shelters
and warned their scoffing neighbors
not to beg admission
when the bombs began to fall.

Somehow we adjusted to M.A.D.
and didn't really notice that we had become mad
and we went about our business day to day,
until the winds of change swept the land
and a minority group demanded civil rights.

Protests disrupted the comfort of the ruling cliques
and the more rabid cliquers brought out the dogs
and they delivered murder and mayhem
to the outspoken intruders,
and couldn't wash them away with water hoses.

When the demands for civil rights
could no longer be ignored
the powers that be needed a distraction
and selected the time tested remedy,
foreign war, but made a bad choice of Vietnam.

It started so small we hardly noticed,
until the automobile executive
brought the benefits of the production line
to military procedures
that sent our children into battle.

Now it doesn't make much sense to me
that we trusted the makers of the Edsel
with our soldiers, but at least they used up
the neglected bombs and shells from WWII
that otherwise would have wasted away.

And the arms manufacturers struck gold
when this restricted war expanded
and expended planes, guns, bullets, meals ready to eat,
all the equipage an army consumes
as it carries out its mission.

Win the hearts and minds of the people,
that is the path to victory (so they say),
but we didn't do a very good job
and we had to destroy them to save them
from the light at the end of the tunnel.

Eisenhower, Kennedy, and Johnson,
each passed on the baton of war,
only Nixon fumbled the transfer
and tried to bluff better poker faces,
until he cashed in our chips in Paris.

What a time Henry K. had in *gay Paree*.
Oops. I don't think we call it gay anymore.
It's important to be politically correct.
He discussed the shape of the table for a year
while the fighting went on . . . and on . . .

Then he argued for another year
about who would sit at the table,
while the fighting went on . . . and on . . .
And in the end we slunk out like the French,
abandoning our allies and the MIAs.

The anti-war foes cackled in triumph.
Legislators discovered new agendas.
The silent majority remained silent.
Our soldiers were blamed for the debacle
and sullenly withdrew to their tents.

And the politicians blamed the troops
who had obeyed legitimate orders,
while Hanoi Jane visited the enemy
and prayed for the death of our children,
yet mom and dad still went to her movies.

Throughout this contradictory land
there are educational institutions
that nurture bitter haters of this land
and comfort some with tenure, while they spew
hatred on the land that nourished them.

We know our system is terribly flawed
as the world is quick to remind us.
But long before we became a nation
the ills that plague mankind already existed,
although that's conveniently forgotten.

So we licked our wounds and put the war behind us.
Oops. It wasn't a war. But it wasn't a police action.
Well, let's call it an intervention then,
and we comfortably watched from the sidelines
as our former allies were reeducated.

Then we got down to the real business
of consuming and outspending the Russkies.
So what if we were confused for a while,
the same soothing voices who lost China sang,
so what if we lost Vietnam, we still have Iran.

Then countries began to fall apart
as imperialist control was removed
from ethnic groups in Europe, Asia, Africa,
once suppressed for the good of the state
now with new found freedom to oppress others.

Little wars flared all over the globe
and some affected us, or our friends,
but we tried not to take them personally,
because that would interfere with business
and divert us from bigger profits.

And our purchase power grew and grew
and our people weren't too unhappy
with the commitment to butter and guns,
as long as there was plenty of butter
and the guns were used somewhere far away.

Then the Soviet Union had a great fall
and not even you-know-who could pick up the pieces,
and the former commies scrambled for their share,
while we comfortably observed from the sidelines
and began to worry what we'd do without them.

The Seeker

I have walked your sagging streets,
American cities,
and watched your decay by day,
felt your despair at night
and howled my helplessness
to the untenanted moon
to change your destructive ways.

Our world grows crowded
and future children
will have survival hopes impaled
on blood-stained Hutu spears
that will sing of slaughter
and deny salvation
to our few remaining visionaries.

When Children are Soldiers

Guerrilla soldiers from the Lord's Resistance Army
kidnapped grade-school children in Uganda
adding to the more than eight thousand abducted,
most of them under the age of sixteen.
Children who escaped said they were forced
to torture, maim, even kill one another.
Once they were psychologically broken,
they were used as sex slaves for other soldiers,
or became vicious fighters themselves.

Young people have been soldiers throughout history,
but lately their numbers have increased,
due to the changing nature of war.
Since the end of the cold war
conflicts between countries
have rarely been fought by their armies.
Most wars today are nationalist, ethnic, or religious,
led by warlords who forget the Geneva Conventions
and appreciate the spread of automatic weapons,
as long as a child can use an AK-47.

Philosophic Ramblings

In the coincidence of life
we postpone death daily,
yet rarely seek higher purpose.

Now that we have been mastered
by the seductive video screen
we are victims of electronics.

Evil conspires with gravity
and pulls us down, down,
as we substitute spectation
for entangling alliances.

The grievances that rasp our hearts
devour the pleasure of our days
and stir seething cauldrons of hate
that will spill on our tomorrows.

Man is the cruelest animal,
exceeding any creature of nature
in torture, mayhem, and destruction.

We are raised in the garden of greed
and become trapped in the ghetto of need.

The unkind earth eats us all.

Death smiles when chill creeps in our bones.

Humanity, our dysfunctional family.

Suffer the Children

To Arla Beck

I do not sleep well at night,
lie contorted in my bed
tormented by the thoughts I dread,
and have been helpless to prevent,
man's crimes against humanity.

Children of the Holocaust,
torn from helpless mothers' arms,
rushed to the oven by the gingerbread man
and no savior came along
to save them from extermination.

Children of the Hutu and Tutsi,
torn from helpless mothers' arms,
starved, stabbed, speared, shot, savagely slain.
Tiny skeletons litter the jungle
and do not reveal their tribe.

Children of American slums
are seldom torn from mothers' arms,
but are abused by uncles, brothers, boyfriends,
who torture them day and night
until the world is no longer right.

In Memoriam: Kitty Genovese

To Mario Biaggi

When you walked home that fateful night
you could not know what awaited you.
Nor could your complacent community
imagine their callous lack of response
when that madman stabbed again and again.
It was not just another urban crime
in the torrent of evil we contrive
that shatters illusions of decency.
When the neighbors refused to help
and didn't rush out to defend Kitty,
they watched from the safety of their windows
the slaughter of a girl, the fraying of society.

Boy Soldiers

When the gunfights in Liberia
for control of downtown city streets
blemished the face of the capital,
leaders did not retire and regroup.
Instead, chiefs of warring militias
decided like other commanders
that the fighting was just too intense
to risk lives of experienced men.

Then the battle for Monrovia
became a bloody all-child affair
quite similar to many battles
in other conflicts around the world,
where children rejected in peace time,
who lacked skills, except in starvation,
suddenly were prominent in war
like their fiercely combatant elders.

In a typical urban firefight
adults took cover in ruined buildings,
or sniped from behind wrecked vehicles
at any living target that moved.
Boys no older than seven or eight
were sent out to dash through risky streets,
making obscene gestures and dancing
in order to draw enemy fire.

Some children fired AK-47s
with the skill of their fearsome elders.
Others launched rocket propelled grenades
with childish glee at loud explosions.
Some kids were happy to play decoy,
dashing through a wild hail of bullets,
carrying toy guns, eager to prove
they were brave and deserved to survive.

No one knows when kids first went to war
and served as pack mules, or water boys,
laborers, human bombs, drummer boys,
and were shot down before they grew up.
They were recruited through kidnapping,
fed drugs in order to calm their fears,
trapped by addiction, or like most boys,
attracted to the power of guns.

Child combatants fight in many lands,
Burma, Sudan, and Guatemala,
Laos, Cambodia, and Peru.
Liberia consumes the most kids,
who fight mostly in civil conflicts,
typically used by rebel forces
opposing current authority
and lost boys have no advocate.

At the end of each day of fighting
a strange and eerie calm may prevail.
Ravaged streets display the evidence
of the toll of brutal child abuse.
Many corpses, small and often frail,
lie in heaps where they fell in battle,
their flesh picked at by carrion birds,
until they're burned to remove their stench.

When warlords prepare for rebellion
they create a patriotic front
to legitimize the heinous crimes
that should horrify humanity.
But too burdened by information
to maintain the fight against evil,
people seek mindless entertainment
that numbs them to the call for action.

In this topsy-turvy world of loss
few resist the seduction of greed
and those who grab the most booty
seek equality with guns.
Somewhere in the nihilistic dream
that exalts those with firepower
there should be safety for homeless youth,
the victims in this destructive scheme.

The comforting sense of belonging
that the war provides to boy soldiers,
most of them orphaned in the conflict,
seduced by the allure of the gun,
who fearlessly go into battle,
miniature troops playing at war,
who panic at loss of their rifles,
no sanction short of death could be worse.

Squads of not-yet-five-foot-tall soldiers
kill like adults on the battlefield,
then break down into uncontrolled sobs
when disciplined for any reason.
Then their fighter friends cannot help them
and there are no laws to protect them
and warlords are quick to expend them
in the nightmare that precedes their death.

There once was a skinny boy soldier
in battle for five of his twelve years,
a child of this mercenary life,
a son of the militia of tears.
He dreamed of a country without war
where people owned too much to destroy,
but he knew it would not be his land,
for he was born to meet a bullet.

Physicists of Detachment

Remote theorists of matter
often ignore passengers on vessel earth
and never warn us this solar step-child,
a coincidence planet that oddly nurtures life,
may soon find much of it dispensable,
especially for ungrateful humans,
who won't give the space-faring derelict
necessary maintenance.

Saga of the Ages

To Paul Kennedy

Nomadic Man
    Crossing plains and deserts,
    first on foot, then horse,
    in search for food, water,
    killing the weak, avoiding the strong,
    no different than the rest of nature.

Agricultural Man
    We don't know who planted the first seed,
    a warrior who couldn't keep up, a genius,
    or slacker seeking the easy life,
    but men discovered plants took time to grow
    and built a city so they could hang around.

Feudal Man
    City dwellers are slicker than country folk
    because they bow their heads more often
    to those who appoint themselves their betters
    and have to endure and survive
    the urban evils man creates.

Renaissance Man
    When they dug up the heritage of the past
    it gave an awful lot of underlings
    new ideas that made them hate the status quo,
    which demanded that artists be artisans
    and diminished their creative value.

National Man
>Then kings and princes set boundaries
>and people were told to uphold them,
>and they forged a new identity
>they were privileged to die for,
>the innovation of the modern state.

International Man
>The needs of the nation are neglected,
>the hopes of the people are forgotten
>by the new men, the electronic men,
>who extend their empires in atoms
>that collide below public awareness.

Lunar Man
>We may not survive long enough to settle
>on your dust-filled rills, already lifeless,
>a model for our plan for Mother Earth,
>who cannot resist our insane assaults
>on our air, water, future.

Monstrous Abuse

To Kofi Annan

The proliferation
of brutal civil wars,
with compulsory recruitment
of children for combat
added another abuse
to the endless abuses
devised for our children.
Thousands of children
are forced into battle
after learning the lessons
of terror and rule of the gun.
They are victims and victimizers,
kidnapped and drugged,
forced to kill their families
so they cannot return home.
Girls are abducted
then used as sex slaves.
Governments or guerillas,
equally without shame,
violate the covenant
to preserve our young.
Demobilization
lets an adult soldier
return to civilian life.
Child soldiers,
robbed of family and education
know no other life
and have been abandoned
by the community of man.

Daughters of Cambodia

She giggled for a moment,
the skinny, twelve-year-old girl-child
of sparkling eyes and gleaming teeth.
Her laughter drowned the obscene grunts
of the man on her younger sister.

The brothel owner strutted by,
a scowling woman in her twenties,
heart missing beneath traditional garb,
carefully guarding her property.
She paid good money for the girls.

The brothel owner paused and smiled
and praised the virtues of the child,
baring her left breast, well, the nipple
of what will become her left breast,
if she survives to maturity.

The customer calmly haggled
while the owner praised the child's body,
claiming eight dollars was not too much
for a girl who just recently
had lost her prized virginity.

But her virginity was lost
many and many a year ago
in a brothel far from the sea,
when her father sold her to servitude,
to endure men's lust for a fee.

Now she labors till her debt is paid,
or until they know that she has AIDS.
She can't escape for she'll be caught,
severely beaten, starved, cruelly forced
to have sex with abusive men.

This child is one of tens of thousands
slaving in the sex plantations
of the growing cottage industry,
the Asian brothels of China,
India, Thailand, the Philippines.

The child prostitutes of Asia
sustain the evil appetites
for brutal molestation and rape,
forbidden at home to lawless men,
who post their lust on the Internet.

Daughters of Cambodia
and other Asian lands,
you are unwilling playthings
of brothel keepers' greed
and sick, consumer lust.

When sex tours started in Japan,
Korean and Taiwanese brothels
cheerfully accepted the money
that let Koreans and Taiwanese
tour Manila and Bangkok brothels.

So Asia's economic boom
brings more babies to prostitution,
some sold by desperate parents,
others kidnapped off the streets,
as an ill wind blows from the east.

The rise of Asian prosperity
breeds new markets for human flesh,
increases appetites for children,
obeys laws of supply and demand
and violates all morality.

When AIDS the viral killer came
the men of Asia responded
using younger and younger children,
who were less likely to be infected
with the spreading sexual gift.

So AIDS the viral killer goes
quickly from country to country,
with children sold across borders,
while customers shop from place to place,
then leave with a final souvenir.

And in the east the Asians go
and put the blame on G.I. Joe,
but all the sins were surely there
before Americans would share
their native vices with the world.

Shanghai, Hong Kong, Hanoi,
cities famous years ago
for traffic in the flesh of youth,
blamed on wretched poverty,
yet profit increases slavery.

G.I. Joe and westerners
helped build the brothels of Asia,
when their military bases
crammed full of rich, horny soldiers,
spread the wealth and sustained the trade.

And what of the children's suffering,
smuggled across Vietnamese borders
and other lands, victims of collapse
of strict commie ideology,
and the demands of the flesh trade.

The buyers of virginity
are foreigners, generally
newly prosperous Chinese,
for the superstitious Chinese claim
sex with virgins makes them young again.

And the children are always frightened,
desperate, debauched, diseased,
vaginas so easily torn,
leading to sores and the bleeding
that promotes HIV breeding.

Most men prefer the younger girls
because they're easily abused.
The older girls can set a price
and may even set conditions
that younger girls cannot demand.

Little girls learn the curse of sex
when they're forced to perform for others.
A girl cannot make a grown man
use a condom when he refuses,
then gives AIDS to the child he uses.

In a brothel in Cambodia
for a five-hundred-dollar fee,
a girl lost her virginity,
a onetime opportunity
for a bargain hunting buyer.

A helpless child speaks for her sisters.
"My life no longer matters,
nobody seems to care.
It's better for me to die.
Cambodia won't cry."

High Brow Is Safer

In our land
the yahoos come and go
as blind to reason
as the buffalo.
Though not as primitive
as Goth, Hun, or Vandal,
the rampaging hordes
have become a public scandal.
Riding personal watercraft,
or mounted on a snowmobile,
they assault our waterways
and trash parks with sordid zeal.
As ancient cultures lived in dread
of nomad's seasonal migration,
springtime brings a shudder
from nature in anticipation.
It almost makes a poet yearn
for literary pretensions,
that do no harm and fit right in
to our cultural conventions.

Questions About the Cold War

Brrr. Why is it so cold?
Why didn't Truman use antifreeze?
Who really started it, us'uns or them'uns?
When did silos start storing missiles instead of grain?
What lunatic dreamed up M.A.D.?
Where do unused bomb shelters go?
How did we end up with global warming?
If we really won the cold war, why are we so tepid?
Do some of us dream of the tense old days?

Child Abuse

Don't strike a child
furiously
if you think he gives you
some delusional
rhyme, reason, pretext, subtext,
of indescribable collusion,
an invitation to contusion
in an unwarranted intrusion
of his sovereignty.

The statute of limitations
for parental violations
has never quite expired
when children select
the personal gift
of automatic weapons.

My Country

Across this once flourishing land
corporate entities despoil
the water and the air we breathe.
Masters of anonymity
until captured in wrongdoing,
then they're flayed in the media,
but exposure doesn't stop them.
Another felon replaces them,
the sacrifice to public wrath.
Brief is the public memory
and we're encouraged to forget
all ills by unctuous newscasters,
who outdo bread and circus
erasing concern with diversion
for twenty-four/seven brainwash,
until we accept anything
our economic masters do,
regardless of the consequence.
So they buy pollution credits
from less efficient polluters
in order to keep polluting
and we accept this lunacy,
as we accept other madness
with indifferent resignation.

Charles Bukowski

If poets are birds,
you are a seagull,
a dirty old herring gull,
crudest of the flock.
And your raucous voice
squawks louder than other shore birds,
as you urgently feed on what you scrounge,
whether from nature or transients.
Mating is almost as important as eating,
and your lecherous gaze
falls on available birds
who succumb to your vulgar display.
But drinking comes before everything else
and you'll swill just about anything
your filthy beak can dip into.
Yet your grating ways
are quickly forgotten,
redeemed by robust poems
that shatter pretensions,
startle frailer birds
with sensitive insights.

Train Ride II

The wheels roll
screech and throb,
babies cry,
newspapers rustle
like birds on trains,
flocking to destinations.

The train stops,
faces press on windows,
flattened mouths whisper
what's wrong?
What's wrong?
Just another station.

Oh, vehicle of dreams
rushing us north,
or other fixed directions,
our heads recline on seats
as we stifle the yawns
that devour arrivals.

Kinder Capitalism

To Donald Rumsfeld

In the 1930s,
the Soviet Union wasn't happy
because stubborn peasants
cultivated small plots of land,
and were dealt with drastically,
using various methods, including:
one way tickets to Siberia,
imprisonment,
execution,
and for the fortunate,
life on a collective farm,
all dictated arbitrarily
by the will of the state
for the purpose of
improving agriculture.

At the very same time,
in the good old USA,
our weather beaten sharecroppers
were blown off the land,
until all they had to eat
was a bowlful of dust.
Now unlike the Soviet Union,
where big, bad comrades
could dispose of your fate,
here it was the banks,
and once the sharecroppers
were kicked off the land,
they were free to go
wherever they wanted,
and as long as they didn't disrupt,

disturb, distress, discomfort
the rest of the USA,
they were still left
with the personal choice
to suffer and starve
democratically.

At the Shore

The sky is darkening,
faces in the sunset light
glow red.
The beach is quieting . . .
A lone kite soars higher than a gull.
Mother and daughter
dig the last sandcastle.
A small boat races home,
urgent to beat the menacing dark.
The glowering pink sky
growls with the weight
of old Sol going west.
A cool breeze
blows across the boardwalk,
WPA built in 1937.
Joggers and runners
pound the boards,
startling old ladies
with pink hair
and faded lace shawls.
Then evening slides in.
The sky succumbs to sullen red.
Another casual day ebbs away.
Darkness claims the promenade,
and thoughts of drink, dance, and growing lust
propel the tourists to smoke-filled bars,
as the night cycle goes on
to some formless destination,
preparing adornments
before the final funeral.

The Art of War

To Paul D. Wolfowitz

In a strictly local dispute one day,
overmatched Og picked up a handy stick
and bashed his opponent over the head.
Onlookers grunted loudly in surprise
and one primitive hulker grunted foul.
The Mountain Tribe debated the issue
without an immediate conclusion
whether or not Og had broken the law,
which was too complex for quick decisions.
One day the River Tribe attacked the cave
and Og boldly grunted *Follow me, boys*,
and they picked up their sticks and won the day.

One primitive hulker still insisted
that it was cowardly to use a club,
but Og's dazzling triumph was inspiring
and made the healthy brutes ape his methods,
and they dominated the River Tribe,
till Gooma, dreamer of the River Tribe,
grew disgusted with regular defeat,
and during another losing battle
picked up a big rock and threw it at Og.
One primitive hulker quickly cried foul,
but when Gooma the dreamer saw Og fall,
he threw more rocks and his tribe won the day.

One primitive hulker still insisted
that it was cowardly to throw a rock,
but Gooma the dreamer convinced the tribe,
until all of them aped his methods
and they boldly battled the Mountain Tribe.
Sometimes clubbers won and sometimes rockers,

but descendants of Og swore by the club
and offspring of Gooma swore by the rock.
The balance of power remained even,
until a hunting Ogite missed his prey,
and threw his sharpened stick and killed a deer.
They proclaimed him the leader of the tribe.

The offspring of Gooma threw their rocks well
and began to dominate the battles,
till an Ogite thought of throwing his spear
and in the next fight wounded a Goomite.
One primitive hulker quickly cried foul,
but when the other Ogites threw their spears
the disconcerted Goomites fled the field.
The primitive hulker still insisted
that it was cowardly to throw a spear,
but he was scorned, as the Goomites hurried
to find a place with more spherical stones
that could be thrown with more accuracy.

Soon life became very complicated,
for the men lugged spears and stones all day long
in preparation for the next battle
and they were much too busy for hunting.
So the women began to get angry,
because there was no food for the children
and they refused to mate with their menfolk,
until they were given enough to eat.
One primitive hulker quickly cried foul,
but the men assessed the situation
and decided that women should carry
the spears and stones while the men went hunting.

This practical domestic arrangement
allowed the men to continue the war,
although battle was ritualistic.
They fought from a distance so far apart

that only a few fighters got wounded.
One fine day, after spears and stones were thrown,
a surly Goomite still wanted to fight,
and he charged, although he had no weapons.
More Goomites followed him and they grappled
in close combat for the first time in years.
The Ogites weren't prepared for the charge
and fled the field after getting pummeled.

Then the Ogites were in a state of shock
from the beating they recently received,
and when one primitive hulker cried fair,
the tribe became angry and banished him.
A critic was punished for the first time,
but that didn't help the tribe solve the problem
of how to deal with physical assault.
A local dispute over meat ended
when an Ogite picked up his eating stone
and stabbed his neighbor with the sharpened point.
After the shock of the stabbing wore off,
the tribe began practicing how to stab.

Then the very next time the two tribes fought,
after the normal grunting and taunting,
when both sides had thrown all their stones and spears,
the Goomites made the long awaited charge,
and when they got close enough to grapple
they met with an unexpected surprise.
The Ogites pulled eating stones from their pelts
and ferociously stabbed their opponents.
Bleeding Goomites fled as fast as they could,
and a primitive hulker grunted foul,
but the River Tribe licked its painful wounds,
then practiced stabbing with their eating stones.

For hundreds of years tribes fought the same way,
as traditions became deeply rooted.

Since all tribes used the exact same weapons,
victory or defeat was determined
by various intangible factors:
distracting lice bites at crucial moments;
not enough fat consumed the night before;
unfavorable omens in the sky.
The tribes knew that they had to make changes
and requested the makers of pictures
to conceive of some new ways of warfare,
like ambushes, night attacks, booby traps.

Then for centuries war was innovative
and tribes even explored technology,
but the element of surprise faded,
and war was resolved by force of numbers,
and small tribes were compelled to join large tribes.
After that the battles became bigger
and more and more tribesmen were casualties.
Medical services were limited,
as were disability benefits,
so survival was simply determined
by whoever managed to get away
from the battlefield without injury.

For hundreds of years the fortunes of war
swung back and forth between various tribes.
Despite any victories or defeats,
no tribe could establish its dominance.
When one tribe became dangerously strong,
ambassadors from other tribes gathered,
exchanged gifts, and grunted for unity.
When they could overcome their suspicions
of the other tribe's treacherous motives,
ambassadors were able to unite
the tribes, for the temporary purpose
of defeating the foes who threatened them.

One tribe's dominance didn't last very long,
neither did the tribal coalitions.
For hundreds of years the nature of war
was exceptionally predictable.
The most successful technique in battle
was the exceedingly well-set ambush.
When the enemy got wise to surprise,
they made traditional horns-down charges
that primitive hulkers always approved.
The night attack fell into disfavor,
because they couldn't see what they were doing
and it frequently ended in chaos.

Then some primitive hulkers grew bigger
and were able to make fiercer charges
that overwhelmed their weaker opponents.
So for hundreds of years the mammoths won,
until an Ogite held onto his spear
and stabbed his foe before he could grab him.
His fellow tribesmen called him a hero
and they all practiced stabbing with their spears.
The next time the tribes met in battle
the stabbing spearmen were victorious,
and though one primitive hulker cried foul,
the victors continued stabbing with spears.

For thousands of years the fortunes of war
swept back and forth without a decision.
One tribe's totalitarian vision
wasn't strong enough to conquer the rest,
and the usual migrations went on,
until the nearby food was depleted.
Then at a time of a major crisis,
a youngster who had been taming horses
proposed that the whole tribe learn how to ride,
so they could ride long distances for food.
One primitive hulker quickly cried foul,
but the rest of the tribe learned how to ride.

For centuries tribes migrated on horseback,
killing, looting, pillaging, enslaving
boys and women, stealing everything else
that they could carry away on horseback.
Whatever they could not carry they burned.
One tribe grew tired of the brutal assaults
and piled rocks together as barriers,
to prevent horsemen from riding them down.
The very next time the horsemen attacked
they had to dismount to get at their foes,
which gave the defenders an even chance,
and they managed to defeat the horsemen.

The horsemen started attacking the tribes
that hadn't constructed rock barriers,
but soon rumors spread that horses couldn't jump
over rocks, if they were piled high enough.
So previously neglected tribesmen,
who were mocked for having rocks in their heads
for trying to make defensive rock piles,
suddenly became very popular.
The piles of rocks kept the horsemen at bay,
until they learned how to knock down the piles.
Then for many years the horsemen prevailed
and the rock-piling tribes were defeated.

Whenever the horsemen knocked down the rocks
the fearful defenders fled for the hills,
leaving behind their crops and belongings,
and huddled together in freezing caves.
One builder grew tired of bone-chilled nights
and packed the space between rocks with wet mud.
In the morning he tried to move the rocks
and discovered they were stuck together.
It took many men to dislodge the rocks,
and they quickly grasped the basic idea
that filling the space between rocks with mud
made walls that were too strong to push over.

The horsemen began to avoid stone walls
and only attacked the tribes without them,
until everyone learned to put up walls.
Then a frustrated horseman insisted
that it was cowardly to build a wall,
but he was scorned by his fellow horsemen
who had more important things on their minds,
such as how to get past solid stone walls.
The horsemen devised many new techniques
to break down walls that the tribesmen put up.
The tribesmen learned how to defend their walls
and for a while they were victorious.

Then the horsemen re-invented the bow
that their ancestors once used for hunting,
and by making it bigger and stronger,
they were able to shoot arrows further
than defenders could throw spears from the wall.
So the horsemen would shoot down the wall men,
then easily manage to scale the walls.
This disturbed a great number of wall men,
who had grown used to safety behind walls,
and they considered new means of defense,
then decided to try bow and arrow,
which worked, and kept horsemen at a distance.

The horsemen grew desperate to find ways
to break down the stone walls that defied them,
and they began to increase their numbers,
so they could overwhelm the defenders.
This led to battles between the horse tribes
and the losers always joined the winners.
It was during a personal combat,
when a horseman was about to be speared,
that he deflected the spear with his cloak.
Other warriors observed his defense,
and started using thick animal hides
to shield themselves from an enemy's thrust.

The horsemen traveled in enormous hordes
that easily overran small enclaves,
so the defenders gathered more tribesmen
and built bigger walls that held more fighters.
Sometimes they managed to beat back the horde,
which couldn't stay for very long in one place,
since they'd soon run out of food and water,
which would force them to give up the attack.
So the fortunes of war swung back and forth
between the horsemen and the new cities.
When the horsemen couldn't capture the city
in one mad dash, they were forced to ride on.

The battles for the cities grew fiercer,
as the walls became bigger and stronger,
and horsemen tried to develop new ways
to attack cities that resisted them.
City folk also invented new ways
to defend the walls that protected them.
But for both sides strategy was simple,
basically limited to: *There they are*.
Tactics were barely more complicated,
mostly limited to: *Let's go get them*.
So for hundreds of years clever soldiers
were forced to contrive a lot of new tricks.

The horsemen used logs as battering rams,
as they attempted to break down the walls.
The defenders resisted the attacks,
throwing rocks, spears, and pots of boiling oil.
The fortunes of war began to depend
on who could develop better methods
of carrying out a full-scale attack,
and improving the techniques of defense.
Brains now became more important than brawn,
and though courage would always be valued,
the thinker took command of the battles
and firmly established the art of war.

Confession

I declare
the following confession
is uncoerced
and is freely given
as a testament
to the misdeeds of my days.

Now I didn't start the cold war,
since I wasn't even a teenager
when much of the world froze sides.
And I didn't start the Korean not-a-war.
Police action. That's what we called it.
We wouldn't admit we were at war again.

So my crimes began c. 1954,
when I left my teachers for uncle Walt,
who urged me to resist much, obey little.
And I preferred good old uncle Walt,
because the words he spouted sounded better
than the drivel in the classrooms.

So off I went to college, abandoning
the vulnerable high school kids
who went online and became consumers.
It was my fault that they believed in the system,
except for the radicals, who were against
all kinds of stuff, but not for anything sensible.

Then for many years I struggled to learn
what is *right* action and how to take it,
but I couldn't prevent the ills of the world.
My crimes continued until I formed
an organization to help the needy
and others joined me to fulfill this vision.

And we did well and helped many in need,
but we didn't strut our good work in public,
so the government and private funders
didn't appreciate our dedication
and cut funds without thought for the needy,
taking more light from a darkening world.

Peasant's Complaint

Once again the summer has passed
and again the wheat did not grow.
Soon I must go into the town
and tell the local committee
that I have not produced my quota.
Once, some of the committee
were my neighbors, farmers like me.
Now they belong to the party,
and all of them have forgotten
what it's like to work the soil.

Fresh

Thou art fair,
je t'adore,
you be fresh,
how many ways
to say I love you
(Do men say these words
to other men these days?),
and if the vocabulary
differs slightly
from age to age,
it matters not the phrase,
as long as love is served.

Lament

I mourn the days to come
when I will no longer see
a flock of Robins,
that will be eradicated,
like other inconveniences
by remorseless man.

Terrorism

To John Ashcroft

Terror is a disease
that attacks the body natural,
like business or politics,
which we think are normal.

The self-appointed pundits
and the experienced analysts
all tell us glibly
that the cause of terror
is poverty and illiteracy,
but closer scrutiny reveals
that most terrorists
are literate and well-to-do.

Then some experts assert
that terror is caused
by middle-class alienation,
rather than third-world deprivation.

The most popular current theory
is based on the concept of humiliation,
which is cited as the best reason
that self-destructing bombers are recruited.

Terrorists are always outsiders,
urgent to inflict their demands
on non-compliant societies.

Terrorism is as old as man
and it grows out of greed
and the lust for power.

By the time we get to know terrorists
it's much too late to change them,
so the best thing we can do
is to profile them ASAP
and eliminate them PDQ.

President Clinton

Missiles and bombs, bombs and missiles,
are more lethal than epistles.
Stealth planes, B-52s, Tomahawks
(not the legendary hatchets)
rained down upon Saddam Hussein's minions,
a non-refreshing shower of destruction
that distracted our fellow Americans
from an imminent impeachment vote.

The President's impudent crimes
were foisted on the republic,
while the stench of corruption
in the high office in the land
pervaded the capitol district,
permeated the cities and the towns,
polluted the dwindling small farms
and settled in dangerous coal mines.

The day before the House decided
to bring a criminal to trial,
slick Willie ordered an attack
on not-so-innocent Iraq,
which delayed deliberations
of felonious machinations.
But give Bill credit as a man,
he didn't disrupt Ramadan.

Willy Bosket

Willy Bosket,
the most confined prisoner in America,
may be the monster
that the government say he be.
But we only know
what the media want us to know,
that Willy is still alive,
but buried deep, deep, deep
in distant dungeon,
too far removed from scrutiny
to verify his humanity.
If Willy be too bad
to go to work, or school,
or do redeeming social chore,
maybe he should get something worse
than chains, restraints,
deprivations, isolations.
Eligible participants,
employees and residents
of any penal system, anywhere,
could contribute to a contest,
and the winning entry would determine
the fate of Willy.

Ode to Hope

Although we cannot right
all the ills of this world
and suffering will go on
despite our best efforts,
there is still a hope
that on brightest days
we will see tomorrows.

Times Square

Having left you once
42nd street,
not long enough
so your gambling, dope, flesh,
and all the predatory faces,
respirating evil
into the concrete world
have been forgotten,
I returned to smut central,
but did not find
drugs, disease, despair,
just the dancing feet
of digital tourists
tapping away
on sanitized sidewalks.

Confined to . . .

Long tired of pandering
to avarice,
dullness,
stupidity,
I sought a change,
thinking
to escape entombment
in a civilized clime,
forgot, renounced, buried,
hopes, dreams, ambitions
for other gains.
I became a panther
in a gilded cage,
paced
furious, desperate, snarling
from wall to wall,
found no release,
became a plant,
choked by the shade.

Two Hotel Songs

I have listened to
this woman
writhing under me,
caught by the agony
of dripping ecstasies.
Her fluid moan
pushes back
the puke-green walls
of a cheap hotel
and blinds me to the murmurs
passing through the puke-green walls
as the song of our bed
entertains the lonely dwellers
in a drab hotel.

After one love is done
and another is passively lying,
murmurs in the hallway cease
save for creaks and sighing.
The whispering intrusions fade
as all distractions must,
and just the memory remains
of obscene, eavesdropping lust.
We lie there spent and silent,
nothing to be said,
as we listen to the rhythm
of our softly squeaking bed.

Last Flight

The cabin crew,
calm and resolute,
watches while the pressure fails
and the passengers,
camera clad tourists,
gasp for air
when the automatic oxygen containers
don't open automatically.

"This is the captain speaking.
Due to engine failure
we are forced to land
in the ocean.
Do not panic.
I repeat.
Do not panic.
The cabin crew will help you into life rafts.
There is no need for alarm.
Follow the instructions of the flight attendant."

One bottle of tourist rum,
label peeling,
floats on the concealing sea.

Aging Vessel

My brittle skeleton
trapped in the prison
of my festering flesh,
keeps my soul an inmate,
clinging to my splintering bones.

Baal

Your altar is tended with crumbling fingers,
o lost idol of ancient pillars
that invoke nameless victims
bereft of passion,
stained with old blood
in the formless midnights of remembrance.
I pass your dank doorstep of ungreeting,
coursing a madness of timeless hunger,
the dark wanderer of dreary yearning,
trapped in a tattered raincoat.

Two Beach Songs

The beaches of summer
spawn many daughters,
bringing more each year.
They come to sun, swim,
pose on gritty stretches
of scouring sand-
bronzed figures
creative as sculpture,
resonant too.

I recline
leaner and hungrier than Cassius
dreaming of power.
Rarely do I dream of power,
but now,
watching almost naked flesh in undulations,
joining a group of pimpled teens,
I dream of the abuses of power.

Bipolar

Fearful whispers of imagining
follow us down collusive streets
where people strike us
like stilettos,
eager to collect flesh.
Trophies are dear
to blind wanderers
blown though a hurricane world,
who slink in populated corners,
furred against northern nights,
thonged against southern days,
and never cry beware
of fearful imaginings.

Iniquity

My neighbors are a lowly caste
of futile aspirations.
They writhe within crumbling homes,
victims of an unfound foe.
They hate their jobs,
the gritty slum,
unliberating welfare,
anger turned upon their children.
They do not know who to fight,
reminding us of our fragility
without cleanliness, love, pride,
trapping us in degradation.

Explorer

Just before awakening
I dreamed I sailed a tiny ship
across a tempestuous sea
that circled a flat earth
rich in fanciful fables
of fabulous troves of treasure
guarded by demons
brandishing parchments of derision.
Then in a dream within a dream,
a serving girl roused me
from my pauper's bed
and I could tell
from the pitying look on her face
that no word had come
for the land-bound refugee.

Passage

My aches grow more painful
than the festering world
and the Circe of corruption
sings softly in my ear.
Wow! I run down a country road,
chasing a brown and white puppy.
No, that was forgetfulness ago.
Now a bent no one,
once straight and strong as anyone else . . .
I almost remember how fast I ran . . .
But youth is past.
Now I trek the grey road.
I go home and wash
with a gritty cake of soap,
dry myself with threadbare towel,
then whisper goodnight America,
land that I love,
may you awaken a better place
in the hopeful morning.

The New Physics

Fear falls
neither faster, nor slower
in a vacuum
than other emotions,
landing as soft as lead,
as hard as oxygen,
on radioactive imaginings
that cannot prevent
our inevitable decay.

Animal Prisoners

Your stone walls now turned to glass
for birds that neither sing nor fly,
like the wilting eagle
withering from common stares
that stab the captive creatures
with instant demand to be noticed
by callisthenic visitors
intruding on the lifers,
caged beyond appeal.
No ACLU will champion them.
Only the call to higher culture
reprieves the spectated
when the biped brutes
turn their ogling to art,
leaving the lesser beasts
dreaming of fang and claw.

Indignity

A fine mist falls
light as baby's laughter
gurgling
on scurrying
Fifth Avenue ladies
in flowery straw hats,
melting
from ill-bred rain.

The slow rain
hates old dreams
of pink, straw hats
worn by grand dames.
When myths pass dank streets
their old hats melt
from rain's spite.

Delusion

Time marooning me
empireless and alone,
my song an inner growl
of discontent and vengeance,
my foes not paper foes
crushable in a careless squeeze,
but carnivores of desire
knelling doom to expectations
lost in the high rafters,
drowned in the mad swim
to the hope of the horizon
where I will be rescued
by the life raft of destiny.

Stress

Artificial

I sit behind my desk
watching the door.
Who will enter next?
A messenger,
with a memo of doom?
An office cruiser
after my body?
If I lose my job,
what next?

Real

I sit in the cabin
watching the door.
Who will enter next?
A messenger
with a tomahawk of doom?
A fierce beast
after my body?
If the crops fail,
what next?

Democracy In Action

Justice moves
neither swift, nor sure,
inexorable to some,
ponderous
to those it crushes,
like the democratic process
that spares some by accident,
ruins some by intent.

Warning

Finding visions
only at rare times
during wild commotion,
waves bursting
on abandoned beaches,
tranquilizing the terror
of uncharted collisions
with tortured expectations.
Tomorrow spins and spins
a fractured dance,
shedding denials
ominously threatening
red sky at morning.

These United States

What is my country?
Is it the illusions of my youth?
Pilgrims, Valley Forge, Gettysburg,
life, liberty, the pursuit of . . .
the founding fathers,
Washington, Jefferson, Lincoln, Roosevelt.
How simple it seemed in grade school.
But who really owns my country?
Conglomerates, vested interests, exploiters.
Where are the decent men, the just?
Can no one stand up and say: Enough!
Corporations relentlessly consume our future,
diverting us today with cars, clothes, TVs,
as birds, animals, insects dwindle,
as air, water, and earth grow tainted,
who will protect tomorrows?

Alien

If I were an old Jewish man
with hair on my face
I would not sleep on the bus
to Monticello,
but spend the time
in prayer and observation . . .
The greened mountains,
the lush countryside,
a girl's crossed legs across the aisle,
and finally a country club
where people spend the day
hitting little balls with sticks.

Remote Father

In unreachable distances
anesthetically removed
by a hollow heart
I sit alone
and listen to my daughter
crying in darkness.

Metropolis

New York City
awaits its historical moment,
reminding us
with traffic song
of inevitable agony.
Babylon, Berlin, Beirut,
devastated moments
quickly forgotten,
 in the crush of passage
 of foot, hoof, cart, coach, car
that crumbled their ways.

Vast Seas

Humanity,
once again adrift
among your wreckage,
I cross stormy passages,
chartless, more fragile
than sailors of old,
whose tiny wooden hopes
made miraculous transit
on kindless seas.
O voyagers who turn back,
I know your fears.
I recognize your hazards,
but foretell your craven end,
unwilling mariners.

Poems from *Civilized Ways* have appeared in YaSou!, True Poet Magazine, Fullosia Press, Soul Fountain, Struggle Magazine, 971 Menu, Nuvein Magazine, Sentinel Poetry Journal, Clark Street Review, Cerebration Magazine, Decanto Magazine, Poetic Diversity, The Angry Poet, Blue Fred's Kitchen, Remark Poetry, A Little Poetry, Kritya Poetry Journal, Taj Mahal Review, Angel Head, Baby Clam Press, War Journal, Istanbul Literary Review, Thick With Conviction, Unfettered Verse, Chaotic Dreams, Wolf Moon Journal, The Poet's Haven, Blue Fifth Review, The Magpies Nest, Mobius Poetry Magazine, High Altitude Poetry, Ancient Heart Magazine, Poetry Midwest, Lowe Prose & Poetics, Alba, Juice Magazine, Sage of Consciousness Magazine, The Poets Haven, Noneuclidian Café Journal, Conscious Living Poetry Journal, Eleventh Transmission, Merge Poetry Magazine, Kota Press, Ink Sweat and Tears, Poetry Cemetery, AprilMayMarch 777, Munyori Poetry Journal, Carcinogenic Poetry and Poetry Friends, Bleed Me! A River, Bareback Press.

"An Assertion of Poetry" previously published by Wolf Moon Press, 2007.

Some poems in *Civilized Ways* appeared in my chapbook *The Dance of Hate*, published by Calliope Nerve Press.

Some poems in *Civilized Ways* appeared in my chapbook *Mutilated Girls*, published by Heavy Hands Ink.

About the Author

Gary Beck has spent most of his adult life as a theater direc-
tor. He has had numerous published works including *Days
of Destruction, Expectations,* and his novel, *Extreme Change,*
published by Cogwheel Press and *Dawn in Cities, Assault on
Nature,* and *Songs of a Clerk* by Winter Goose Publishing.
Gary has also had several original plays and translations pro-
duced off Broadway, in New York City where he currently
resides.

www.ingramcontent.com/pod-product-compliance
Lightning Source LLC
Chambersburg PA
CBHW031624040426
42452CB00007B/668